T0146631

BACK PATS

LET'S PLAY MAH JONG!

"Well written! Nice cover. I really like it." J. NY

"Congratulations on your publication. Perfect in every way, and fits right into my Mah Jong case. Nice job." S. NS

"Like the simplicity of the instructions." H. SC

"I like the content and pocket size." B. NS

"Thanks for taking the time to write such a great book about the wonderful game of Mah Jong." M. ME

"Well written – great!" M. SC

"I now have my Mah Jong Bible. Carry it in my purse for convenient study." M. NJ

"Hooray for you! What a charming book." M. VT

Let's Play
Mah Jong!

Nancy McKeithan

 www.trafford.com
North America & international
toll-free: 1 888 232 4444 (USA & Canada)
fax: 812 355 4082

THANK YOU
TO

Mrs. Preager, for teaching four children to play Mah Jong many years ago, and for the pleasure that playing the game brought me. I was one of the four.

Leigh Durham, my granddaughter, for her time and patience in transcribing this manual.

Don Durham, baby-sitter, for his assistance in this area.

****

CONTENTS

INTRODUCTION
I Structure of the Game

II Mechanics of the Game

From the Author

       As a long-time player and instructor for many years, of the Ancient Chinese game of Mah Jong, I felt that my observations of the play, the structure, and the reaction of students to the intricate nature of Mah Jong, would be of value to the novice, and those of you who wish to brush up on your game.

       My introduction to, and fascination with Mah Jong, began in childhood when the mother of one of my young friends taught four of us to play. Friends and students aware of my interest in researching the game provided numerous newspaper clippings, early rules, manuals, etc. I am grateful for their thoughtful contributions, as my interest never wanes.

       I found that teaching only the basic structure of Mah Jong was inadequate, developed my own method of instruction that includes the mechanics of playing the game, following the available ancient rules, and sharing what I have learned through my playing experience. This book, written in informal style, contains the information for aiding you, as you become aware of the challenge of playing this ageless game.

SECTION I
Structure of the Game
Pages 1 - 11

Mah Jong – What is it?

Created in China centuries ago, the fascinating game of Mah Jong, the national game of China, continues to draw followers throughout the world. During one era, play was limited to a specific social status. Those outside of this select group risked punishment if caught indulging in the game, with its addictive allure, which continues today.

Basically, four players are required for play. However, two, three, or five may participate. Mah Jong is a game of no partnerships. Even though competitive, an aura of bonding is created among the players.

Mah Jong is played with small tiles, symbolic of nature. The four winds, dragons, flowers, bamboos, circles, and characters. These tiles are made into sets, creating the Mah Jong hand.

Mah Jong is played on the streets of Asian cities, in Mah Jong parlors, in restaurants, and for its relaxing, therapeutic value. One's social demeanor may also be observed while playing this game of skill.

In the past, Mah Jong has had a variety of names: Pung Chow, Ma Cheuk, Game of the Sparrow, Chinese Game of the Four Winds, and today, Mah Jong. It was introduced into America in the early 1920's.

Total absorption in the game is a common occurrence even among veteran players, who are awed by its subtle, irresistible, drawing power. Mah Jong – What is it?

MAH JONG – EQUIPMENT NEEDED

Mah Jong Set
Racks – Four – Each a different color
Dice – Two
Chinese Money – Small, round, plastic chips
Bettor Disc
Table and four chairs
Cover – optional – protects tiles

RULE:
a. Each player has a rack on which the tiles are placed – facing the player.
b. Flowers, all exposed sets of Pungs, Kongs and Chows are placed on top of the rack shelf to be visible to all of the players.
c. The money chips (stake) are stacked on the end of the rack and are used for payment to players at the end of each hand.

NOTE:
If your set includes four blank tiles, you may want to use them for "seat directional tiles" – East, South, West, and North, for each of the seat positions as they move around the table.

No extra tiles? Use four small, smooth, bottle caps. The letters are readily available at hardware and office supply stores.

THE WALL

The Wall is the arena around which the game is played. Creating an exotic touch – it is built of 144 colorful, beautifully engraved, small, "ivory-like tiles" representing the three Suits, Winds, Dragons and Flowers.

Each side of the wall (a square, made up of two tiers of eighteen tiles, thirty-six total) is represented by one of the winds. Moving counter-clockwise around the wall: #1 East, #2 South, #3 West, #4 North. The sequence of these positions and number ALWAYS REMAIN THE SAME, as the East Wind's position moves around the table.

During play, the wall has two distinct sections. The Garden Wall from which replacement tiles for Kongs and Flowers are drawn. And the Open End Wall from which players draw tiles for development of their hands.

Players' turns are made COUNTER-CLOCKWISE. Drawing from the Open End Wall is made in a CLOCKWISE manner.

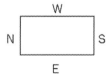

THE TILES

The 144 tiles represent the following:

THREE NUMERAL SUITS
Characters (Cracks)...................... 1-9 Four of each
Bamboos (Bams).......................... 1-9 Four of each
Circles (Dots) .... 1-9 Four of each

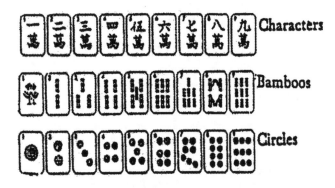

Numeral tiles 2-8 are Simples/Middle tiles.
Numeral tiles 1's and 9's are Terminals; the Honor tiles of the
numeral suits with the higher count than the Simples. These tiles
form the basis for the majority of the hands; providing the options
for numerous combinations of **SETS:** Pungs, Kongs and Chows.
(Refer to page 15.)

THE WINDS – EAST, SOUTH, WEST, NORTH

Known as Letter and Honor tiles, the four winds represent the four
Rounds and the four seat positions at the table, adding increased
count to the score.
Honor Tiles – Four Winds – Four of Each

DRAGONS

Color and Honor Tiles – desirable to have in hand as they double
the count of the player's final score.

    White   Red   Green   Four of Each

FLOWER/SEASON TILES

The Flower/Season tiles (some sets have both) are not used in the
play of the hand. They serve as bonus tiles adding points to the
hand. They fall into two categories: SEAT AND ROUND FLOWERS.

ROUNDS – EAST, SOUTH, WEST, NORTH

Mah Jong is played in Rounds. Each Round and seat position has ONE of the four winds as a prevailing wind and is played in the following manner:

a.   1st four hands of play – Round #1 – East Wind
b.   2nd four hands of play – Round #2 – South Wind
c.   3rd four hands of play – Round #3 – West Wind
d.   4th four hands of play – Round #4 – North Wind

At the end of the round, the next round begins with players casting the dice for the East position and play continues in the usual manner; drawing and discarding tiles until Mah Jong occurs. This procedure is followed for EACH of the four rounds.

RULE: Four completed hands   = 1 Round
                     Four Rounds (16 hands) = 1 Game

WINDS AND PLAYERS
RULE:
a.   Each of the four players must serve as East, the lead position, a minimum of ONE TIME before a round can be completed.
b.   If East Mah Jongs in excess of one time, more than a minimum of four hands will make up the round. These extra hands do not count roundwise. The seat positions remain the same.

c. If East DOES NOT Mah Jong, the seat positions shift with South becoming East by rotation, in a counter-clockwise move.

d. With a winner, hands are counted, tiles turned face down, shuffled, and the wall is rebuilt. All seat positions shift. A new hand begins.

e. During play, if the Garden Wall is depleted, the adjacent wall becomes the garden wall in the same manner as the original one.

Note in the following illustration how the SEAT positions move around the table during play of a round.

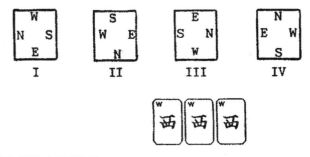

WINDS AND SCORING

If it is the #3 West Round and you have a pung or kong of west winds, the score will be doubled for having the "round Wind" in your hand. This would apply to ANY player.

If YOU are SEATED in the #3 West seat, the score would be doubled again for having your SEAT wind.

FLOWERS AND SCORING

Each seat position at the table has a specific number – East #1, Sout #2, West #3, North #4. Each flower has a number that corresponds to the number of these positions and the Rounds.

South #2 seat - #2 flower. Hand count will be doubled if this flower is drawn. If both #2 flowers are drawn, the count will be doubled twice.

a.   The flower tiles consist of eight.
b.   They comprise two sets numbered 1234-1234, with numerals in two different colors or designs. This will vary with Mah Jong sets.
c.   Upon drawing, all flowers are displayed on the rack shelf, and a replacement tile is drawn from the Garden Wall. The hand will now have the normal complement of thirteen tiles.
d.   At the start of the game all flowers are replaced in rotation: East 1st, South 2nd, West 3rd, North 4th.

JOKERS – Your Mah Jong set may include Jokers. Under the rules of this book they are not used.

ROUND FLOWERS

Each of the four Rounds, representing the four Winds, has its own prevailing flower.

> #1 – East Round .... #1 Flower
> #2 – South Round .... #2 Flower
> #3 – West Round .... #3 Flower
> #4 – North Round .... #4 Flower

The score of a player drawing the #2 flower during the 2nd round would be doubled. If a player drew both of the #2 flowers during this round, the score would be doubled twice.

FLOWER GARDEN/BOUQUET

The Flower Garden is a run (1234) of four flowers of the same numerical color or design, drawn by one player.

a.   This run must be declared when drawn. A late declaration will not be honored.
b.   Each player will pay 1,000 points to the lucky one.
c.   The "run-tiles" do not have the four point count and are discarded after payment.

RULES

A word about rules; the game cannot be played without them! All moves or actions in Mah Jong are governed by specific rules and are NOT to be altered in any manner that will affect the mechanics of the play, count of the hand, or any other aspect of the game.

Throughout this manual, you will find that each action is accompanied by the appropriate ruling.

OPTIONS

a.   Hand point limit – suggested 500. May be any agreed upon amount.
b.   Flower tiles may or may not be used. If NOT used, hand limit should be reduced 100 to 200 points.
c.   The stake – suggested 8,000 points for all players, with group agreement.
d.   KITTY – left to the discretion of the players.
e.   Number of hands played – unlimited.
f.   Use of Special Hands – group agreement. Mah Jong may be limited to just the basic hand. Any Special Hands used must be familiar to all players.

ROTATION -- HOW IT WORKS

In order to minimize confusion in playing, the method of rotation is used throughout the game, and is a must in:

a. Casting the dice.
b. Selection of East Wind.
c. Breaking the wall.
d. Taking turns.
e. Drawing the hands.
f. Drawing for initial flower replacements.
g. Drawing tiles during the play of the hand.
h. Paying the winner at the end of the hand.
i. Payment settlement among other players.

On occasion when a pung or kong is called, a player may lose a turn; however, the play will continue in rotation.

At the end of the hand when payment is made, the players pay each other in rotation. The winner is paid first, and so on around the table in the same manner as a turn. Turns are made counter clockwise. The tiles are drawn clockwise.

SECTION II
Mechanics of the Game
Pages 15 - 62

MAH JONG TERMS & SETS

Mah Jong has its own language or terminology that must be used during play for the following purpose:

a.   To alert players to the play being made by another player.

b.   The term pung or kong will alert the players to the number of tiles that will be available for THEIR USE.

c.   Mah Jong call – a winner – end of hand. When calling for a discard, these terms must be used – Pung – Kong –   Chow – Mah Jong.

TERMS:

PUNG   (set) – Three same suit Numeral tiles   –   444

           (set) – Three same suit Wind tiles   –   NNN

           (set) – Three same color Dragon tiles   –   RRR

EXP.   Exposed pung requires a pair in the hand and the discard from another player. Must be exposed on rack.

CON.   The three like tiles are drawn and kept concealed in the hand.

KONG   (set) – Four same suit Numeral tiles   –   4444

           (set) – Four same suit Wind tiles   –   NNNN

           (set) – Four same color Dragon tiles   -   RRRR

EXP.   Exposed kong requires three in hand and the discard from another player. Must be exposed on the rack with the fourth tile face up, on top of the other three tiles.

CON.   A concealed kong requires three in hand and the fourth tile drawn from the wall. This set is placed on the rack with one tile, face down, on top of the other three tiles.

RULE: If you have an EXPOSED pung on your RACK and DRAW the matching fourth tile, this may be made into a EXPOSED KONG. The EXPOSED pung on the rack CANNOT be made into a kong by the DISCARD from another player.

If you have a concealed kong of numeral tiles (in your hand) it may be used as a pung, three tiles, and one tile as part of a chow, making two sets of the required four for Mah Jong. WHEN A CONCEALED KONG IS USED IN THIS MANNER, YOU DO NOT DRAW A REPLACEMENT TILE FROM THE GARDEN WALL. Discard in the usual manner.

A Kong may be used as two pairs (in hand) when playing one of the Special Hands. A replacement tile is not required.

Kong, unless used as part of a concealed set, requires the drawing of a replacement tile from the Garden Wall.

CAUTION: If another player should Mah Jong, a kong in your hand would be counted as a pung – losing the higher count.

CHOW: A run or sequence of three numeral tiles.
>   Open End – 456   Closed End – 123-789
>   Open – (3)456(7)   Closed – 123(4) – (6)789

When possible – use the open end method. It will enable you to draw to either end of the run. The closed end will restrict the draw.

RULE:

a. One chow may be used as a substitute for a set in the basic hand.
b. A chow made from a discard MUST come from the player on the LEFT.
c. A chow tile needed for Mah Jong may come from the discard of ANY player.
d. A chow may be made from a DRAWN tile.

PAIR/PILLOW

a. Two same color Dragon tiles – red
b. Two same suit Numeral tiles – 77
c. Two same letter Wind tiles – SS

MAH JONG

Requires four sets of LIKE tiles of any suit, winds, or dragons plus a pair of any suit tiles, winds or dragons.

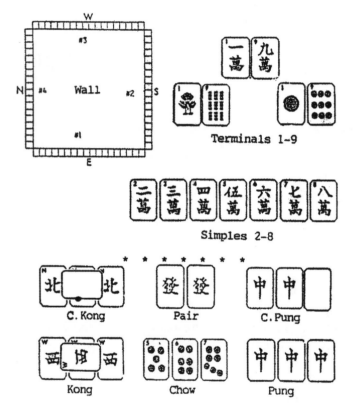

Terminals 1-9

Simples 2-8

C. Kong   Pair   C. Pung

Kong   Chow   Pung

BASIC MAH JONG HAND

The basic Mah Jong hand is made up of four sets of three LIKE tiles, plus one pair of LIKE tiles.

The PLAYING hand is made up of thirteen tiles with fourteen being required to make Mah Jong.

A sequence or run of three numeral tiles may be used as a substitute for one of the sets.

It is imperative that the three types of hands are understood, as they form the basis for playing the game with its variety of combinations.

a. ONE SUIT of ALL numeral tiles with NO winds or dragons. Three doubles of score.
b. Numeral tiles in ONE SUIT with winds and/or dragons. Doubles the score.
c. MIXED SUIT HAND with two or more suits with or without winds and dragons. No double.

NOTE: ONE SUIT hands have a higher count than the mixed hands. Refer to counting.

OBJECT OF THE GAME: To Mah Jong with one of the basic hands, or one of the Special Hands.

One suit hand.

One suit with honors.

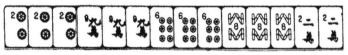

Mixed suit hand.

****

CHINESE TERMS
No Mah Jong – Pin-Chui!
Mah Jong – Woo! I won. Sic-Woo – To Win!
Pung – Pon.   Gan – Concealed
Kong – Kan.   Um Kong – Conc.   Hoi-Kong – Exp.
Chow – Chi
Pair – Ma Cheuk – The Eyes.
One Bamboo – Head of the Bird.
One Bamboo – The Bird of Intelligence.
"Stale Hand" – too few tiles.
"Foul Hand" – too many tiles.

PLAYING THE HAND

Playing the hand involves the following action:

a. Building the wall
b. Selection of East Wind
c. Breaking the wall
d. Drawing the hands
e. Arranging the hands
f. Drawing and discarding
g. Going Mah Jong

ACTION: Building the Wall

RULE: All wall tiles are positioned face down on the table and mixed. The players build a two-tier wall of eighteen tiles each, in front of their rack. These four walls will form a square in the center of the table.

ACTION: Selection of East Wind – the leadership position for the hand.

RULE:

a. Each player, in rotation, counter clockwise – throws the dice.
b. The highest throw becomes East Wind, the #1 seat.
c. Player to the right of East becomes South Wind #2, West Wind #3, North Wind #4.

ROLE OF EAST WIND

ACTION: Leadership for the East position in acquired by the highest throw of the dice made by the four players.

RULE: East Wind
a.   Always – opens the game by casting the dice to designate which of the walls will be broken, and where.
b.   Always – draws the first four tiles.
c.   Always – draws first for any flowers.
d.   Always – discards the first tile to start the game.
e.   Always – pays double and receives double pay.
f.   East Wind may Mah Jong in succession until another player wins the hand. Then the seat position must shift to the player on the right, South Wind. The players do not move, only the "seat" positions shift.

This procedure is followed by each of the East players for the four hands of the round – and all four of the rounds.

SEAT POSITIONS
RULE:
a.   When a player other than East Mah Jongs, the wind positions shift. East moves to South, South to West, West to North and North to the former East position.
b.   When a hand ends with no Mah Jong, wind seat positions shift in the same manner as above.

ACTION: Breaking the Wall

RULE:
a. East throws the dice; the number indicating which wall will be broken and where.
b. East #1, will count around the table #2, #3, #4, until the number thrown on the dice is reached. On occasion, it will be necessary to count around the table several times.
c. The player in this seat position counts in from the RIGHT end of the wall to the number of stacks (2 tiles) designated by the dice numbers.
d. These two tiles are removed and placed side-by-side on top of the RIGHT wall. The bottom tile placed first, the top tile placed second. The second tile is always drawn first in replacing a flower or kong tile.
e. This RIGHT wall becomes the Garden or Flower wall from which flower and kong replacement tiles will be drawn.
f. The LEFT wall is the open end wall from which tiles will be drawn for the play of the hand.
g. The player sitting in this position will angle the wall into the center of the table for easier accessibility.

NUMERICAL BREAK OF THE WALL

East	–	Breaks on a throw of 5 and 9
South	–	Breaks on a throw of 2, 6, 10
West	–	Breaks on a throw of 3, 7, 11
North	–	Breaks on a throw of 4, 8, 12

DRAWING THE HANDS

ACTION: The four hands are now drawn.
a.   A hand consists of thirteen tiles. Fourteen for East Wind, one extra to be used for discard in opening the game.
b.   East will draw the first four tiles (two stacks of the two tier tiles) from the end of the LEFT wall.
c.   South, West and North, in this order, will draw four tiles.
d.   When each player has drawn twelve tiles (three stacks of four tiles), East will draw the first and third (fourteen total) tiles to complete the hand. South, West and North in turn will draw their thirteenth tile.
e.   A hand must always be accountable for thirteen (13) tiles, including those in the hand and sets exposed on the rack. Kongs count as three (3) even though made up of four (4) tiles.
f.   The LEFT wall is the open end wall from which tiles will be drawn for the play of the hand.

CAUTION: Immediately after drawing hand tiles including flower replacement tiles, COUNT YOUR HAND! Any error in the number drawn must be corrected before the first tile is discarded. Otherwise this might cause a penalty.

Any tiles inadvertently exposed in drawing, must be take by the errant player, rather than their own. The next player continues the draw.

ARRANGING THE HANDS

ACTION: Players place tiles on rack, facing them and arrange by: Suits, dragons, pungs, kongs, chows and pairs.

RULE: Flowers are exposed on top of the rack, face up, for replacement prior to the opening of the play. East will draw FIRST, followed by South, West, and North – in rotation.

ALL FLOWERS must be replaced and the tile drawn from the Garden/Flower wall.

THE PLAY BEGINS

ACTION: Lead off...

a. East discards the first tile. This hand will now contain thirteen tiles; the same number as in the other three hands.
b. When discarding, the player identifies the tile by suit and numeral (5 Bamboo), Wind letter (N), and Dragon color.
c. The discarded tile is placed face up on the table, and becomes available to the other players.
d. If the discard is needed, any player may immediately call Pung, Kong, Chow, or Mah Jong, whichever may be relevant.
e. The two matching tiles from the hand will first, be placed on the rack, and the needed discard will be added to complete the set.

f. The player then discards an unwanted tile from the hand.
g. If the tile is unclaimed, it becomes a dead tile and is no longer
    available.

NOTE: YOU DO NOT HAVE TO WAIT YOUR TURN IN ORDER TO CALL
         FOR A DISCARD OR TO MAH JONG.

ACTION: Following the lead of East, the other players in turn,
counter clockwise, will continue to draw from the Open End Wall,
and discard tiles until a player has the required sets, a completed
hand, and announces Mah Jong.

RULE:
a. Each time a tile is added to the hand a discard must be made.
b. When drawing a wall tile, the tile TOUCHED by the player, must
    be taken. It cannot be exchanged for a discarded tile, even
    though the latter is preferable.
c. If a player exposes a tile while drawing, that tile must be taken
    rather than the one the player would have drawn.
d. Any tiles accidentally exposed during play, are buried in another
    section of the wall.
e. If all wall tiles have been depleted and no Mah Jong has been
    called, this is a Wall Game or a Dead Hand.
f. Hands are not counted. Tiles are turned face down, shuffled,
    wall rebuilt, and the seat positions shift. A new hand begins.

DISCARDS – CALLS AND LATE CALLS

RULE:
a. If the next player has drawn a wall tile and has it in their hand, and there is a delayed pung/kong/chow call, the DISCARDED tile is dead. The call is "too late."
b. If a player is "about" to draw from the wall, the tile is replaced. The call will be allowed.
c. Discarded tiles must be claimed immediately upon becoming available.
d. A pung call requires a pair (2) of the same tiles as the discard.
e. A kong call requires a set of three (3) of the same tiles as the discard.
f. A chow call requires a run of two (2) same-suit number tiles. The discard will be the third tile needed to complete the set.
g. For Mah Jong – the discarded tile may be any tile needed to complete the hand consisting of the required four sets and a pair.

DISCARDS – ERRORS

ACTION: If a player TAKING a discard makes an incorrect set and discards, the error cannot be corrected. No Mah Jong allowed.
If the player detects the error, it may be corrected prior to discarding without a penalty.

DISCARDS & TILE PRECEDENCE

ACTION: When two players call for the same tile.

RULE:
a. The tile needed for a Pung takes precedence over a Chow.
b. The tile needed for a Kong takes precedence over a Chow.
c. A tile needed for Mah Jong has priority over a Pung, Kong, or Chow.
d. When two players need the same tile for Mah Jong, the player nearest to the RIGHT of the DISCARDER has priority.

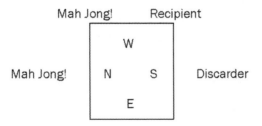

MAH JONG!

ACTION: Arriving at Mah Jong by two methods.

When a player has completed a hand consisting of the requirements of one of the basic hands: Four sets of three tiles and one pair. Total 14 tiles.

When the required combination of tiles for any of the Special Hands has been met.

RULE:
a. When a player declares Mah Jong all play stops.
b. The winner exposes the hand on the rack for observation by the other players.
c. The other three players DO NOT EXPOSE THEIR HANDS until it has been determined that the Mah Jong call is correct.
d. If correct, players place their incomplete hand on their rack for counting and scoring.
e. If the call is incorrect, and no other hand has been exposed, the play continues in the usual manner. (Refer to penalties)
f. Players COUNT THEIR OWN HAND!

CAUTION: The Mah Jong declarer should review the hand for any possible errors before exposing it on the rack. This would avoid a possible costly penalty.

COUNTING AND SCORING
ACTION: Mah Jong has been declared
RULE:

a.   Winner will be paid first, full value of the hand.   DOES NOT PAY
      ANYONE!
b.   Players place their entire hand on rack and count every
      combination that is countable.
c.   Only the winner is entitled to the twenty (20) point bonus for
      Mah Jong.
d.   After the count of sets, flowers, etc. has been made, the
      amount is doubled by any doubles held in the hand, giving the
      final score.
e.   The score is displayed in front of each rack by using the
      appropriate numeral tiles. The other players pay each other
      accordingly. The lower and higher paying the difference in the
      scores.
f.   If the hand limit is 500 points, any score ABOVE that amount
      reverts to 500.
g.   Two players having the same score - Push.
h.   East Wind will pay and receive double pay.
i.   Hands will remain on racks until all payments have been
      verified and made. Pay in rotation.
j.   Errors in scoring cannot be corrected after payment has been
      made.
k.   When the FINAL HAND has been played and all payments
      made, the chips are removed from the racks. Players will
      spread their stake in front of their rack and count the total
      amount to determine the player with the highest score.

BASIC COUNT & SCORE

ACTION: The basic count is made up of the sets and individual tiles on the rack at the end of the hand.

Starting with Mah Jong, if you were the winner, count all flowers, sets and pairs. Add this up to determine your basic or hand count.

NOTE: A DRAWN tile that makes a pung for Mah Jong entitles the set to be counted as a concealed set. WHY? If you were NOT going to Mah Jong, the drawn tile would have made a CONCEALED pung in your hand.
REVIEW YOUR HAND FOR ANY COUNT MISSED. ASK YOURSELF THE FOLLOWING QUESTIONS:

DO I HAVE?
a. The Round Flower -   #1, #2, #3, #4?
b. My Seat Flower -   #1, #2, #3, #4?
c. The Round Wind -   East, South, West, North?
d. My Seat Wind -   East, South, West, North?
e. Have I included all doubles in my hand?
f. Have I doubled the count of all CONCEALED SETS in my hand?

Now, go back and take any doubles. This will be the score that you will declare.

REMINDER: The limit is 500 points. East receives the double payment of 1,000 points.

SCORING SHEET

ITEMS	POINTS
Mah Jong	20
Flowers	4

PUNGS	EXP.	CON.
2's – 8's	2	4
1's & 9's	4	8
Winds & Dragons	4	8

KONGS		
2's – 8's	8	16
1's & 9's	16	32
Winds & Dragons	16	32

PAIRS		
1's & 9's	2	2
Winds & Dragons	2	2

CHOW	0	0

MEMORIZE THE SCORING & DOUBLING SHEET

DOUBLES

FLOWERS

Own Seat Flower .... 1 double
Round Flower .... 1 double

WINDS Pungs/Kong
Seat Wind .... 1 double
Round Wind .... 1 double

DRAGONS
Pungs & Kongs .... 1 double

HANDS

All one suit .... 3 doubles * * *
One Suit, winds &/or dragons ...... 1 double *
Mah Jong – concealed .... 1 double (Basic Hand)
Mah Jong tile drawn from Wall ..... 1 double
One (1) tile needed to Mah Jong
 with a one suit hand .... 1 double

<u>8,000 POINT STAKE</u>

4	Counters	-	1,000 each	-	4,000
6	Counters	-	500 each	-	3,000
9	Counters	-	100 each	-	900
10	Counters	-	10 each	-	100

(Stake may be any amount.)

PAYMENT

The money chips are in multiples of ten. Scoring is converted to the nearest common denominator.

      Score of 1-9 – 10 points
      Score of 12 points reverts to 10.
      Score of 16 points – 20.

West Wind was the winner – paid FIRST.
North and East settle the differences between their high and low scores.
East and South settle their scores.
South and North settle their scores.

North - 80 points
East -   <u>20</u> points
        60 – East Wind pays double – 120 points.
South - 30 points
East -   <u>20</u> points
        10 – East Wind pays double – 20 points.
North - 80 points
South - <u>30</u> points
        50 – South pays North – 50 points.

NOTE: On occasion, a player will run out of chips and may borrow from one of the luckier players. If not repaid prior to the final game, this amount will be added to the final score of the lender. No extra chips are added to the stake after the play begins.

COUNT PRACTICE

You do not need a Mah Jong set in order to make sets of the tiles in learning to count.

Take paper and pencil, use any numeral tiles; letters to identify Dragons and Winds. Make a basic hand and count the sets.

```
555-333-RRR-678-11    = 10 point count
 (2)  (2)  (4)  (0)  (2)   = 20 point score with double
```

Now, check to see if you have any doubles. What SET would double your count?

Ans. The pung of Red Dragons. Honor tiles.

Let's try another hand. You're East Wind!
```
 (B)  (B)  (H)  (B)  (B)
999-222-EEE-666-44 = 12 points. Reverts to 10.
 (4)  (2)  (4)  (2)  (0)
```

NOTE: This is a ONE SUIT hand – 4 sets + pair, all Bams and a set of East Winds. How many doubles? Two.

Sets – all one suit   –   1 double
East's seat wind   –   1 double
Score –   10 points   X   1 double = 20 points
            20 points   X   1 double = 40 points

Your total score (40) is placed in front of your rack, using numeral tiles.

This exercise is an excellent method of learning the Special Hands. When you make them, you will find them easier to remember when you're playing with the tiles.

> Sequence Hand – one suit run plus five odd honors (one of each).
> 123456789 – N, S, W, G, R

This is a CONCEALED – LIMIT hand, meaning that you would have to draw all of the tiles with the exception of the last one needed for Mah Jong. The score is the 500 point limit, if this is the limit for all hands agreed upon by the players.

Try it – you'll soon find count and scoring a breeze!

Seven Pair Hand – 11-77-99-33-EE-NN-RR. May be mixed or all one suit.

DOUBLING – THE SANTA CLAUS OF MAH JONG

What is doubling? The use of specific tiles and makeup of hands that will double the basic count. It is imperative that you understand the doubling process and the sets of tiles which achieve this. Otherwise, it would be detrimental to the count of the hand in playing and discarding.

The HIGH count Honor tiles – Winds and Dragons
The APPROPRIATE bonus tiles – Flowers

DOUBLING: Pung or Kong of a player's seat wind will double the score. Each seat position has a dominant wind (#4 position – North Wind); any drawn North Wind tiles should be retained in the hand for a possible pung or pair.

DRAGONS:	(one color) Pung or Kong will double the score of ANY player.
WINDS:	A Pung or Kong of the ROUND wind will double the score of ANY player.
NOTE:	A PAIR of winds or dragons WILL NOT double the score.
FLOWERS:	Drawing YOUR SEAT flower -#1, #2, #3, #4, will double the score. If you draw both of the same number of the seat flowers, your score will be doubled twice.

Each seat position has a dominant flower.

ROUNDS: For a double, the Round flower must be the
                     appropriate number of the round - #1, #2, #3, #4.

NUMERAL TILES:
DOUBLES:
a.   All ONE SUIT with winds and/or dragons.
b.   All ONE SUIT with no winds or dragons.
c.   "One away" (one tile needed for Mah Jong) with a ONE SUIT
     hand when another player calls Mah Jong.
d.   Drawing Mah Jong tile from the Garden Wall.
e.   Mah Jong with a CONCEALED BASIC HAND.
f.   Mah Jong all Honor Hand.

NO numeral tile pungs or kongs will entitle you to a double. The 1's
and 9's are known as the honor tiles of the numeral tiles (terminals)
and have the same count as the other honor tiles, but not for
doubling the score.

You do not have to Mah Jong to attain credit for any doubles in your
hand.

HAND DEVELOPMENT

Your hand is drawn and you are now staring at thirteen tiles wondering how to play them. Let's look at what you are holding:

a. One long suit? With five or more numeral tiles, try to develop a "one suit" hand. Keep any winds and dragons for possible pairs and doubles.

b. Try one of the Special Hand Sequence hands.

c. Holding three or four pairs? A seven pair hand may be in the offing (Special Hand).

d. Three short suits with two or more winds? Try the special Windy Chow hand or one of the special hands that would adapt to what you are holding.

e. Unusual number of Honor tiles? Try for one of the all-honor-hands. Discard all simples.

f. Two long suites? Try 1-7 in any two suits, or seven pairs in two suits. ALL of the pairs MUST be in the SAME TWO SUITS. The honor tiles cannot be used and are discarded early in the game.

g. Pair hands are not always easy to complete. With a number of pairs, you're set up for a basic hand to "pung" your way out in a hurry. Winning is better than paying!

NOTE: Become familiar with these hands until you can easily recognize the potential of what you are holding. If you have a Mah Jong set, make up the hands and practice them.

Remember to "go for count" and get every possible point from the hand. Be selective in the tiles that you keep, and be aware of the value when discarding them.

Example: You have to make a discard from one of two sets: 444-999. Which? Hope you chose 444.

The basic hand is always there. You may have to draw several times before it begins to take form.

* * * * * * * * * * * * *

Learn at least one of the hands in each category.

Sequence hands	-	Numeral tiles and Honors
Mixed Hands	-	Numerals, Winds and Dragons
Honor Hands	-	Honors and Terminals
Pair Hands	-	All tiles
Chow Hands	-	Numeral Suits

COUNT - DRAWING AND DISCARDING

ACTION: Playing the hand involves two types of action; drawing and discarding. What to KEEP and what to discard.

Keep in mind that you're going for "high count." Your pay out to other players will be less, maybe zero, even though you did not Mah Jong.

"Low Count" – you may end up paying everyone. If you should Mah Jong, you're in the chips, as everyone will have to pay you, even though the amount will be small. Your stake has been saved!

WHAT TO DO:
a. YOUR MUST LEARN THE VALUE OF THE NUMERAL TILE SETS. SIMPLES AND TERMINALS as their value will determine which sets to break up for making a discard.
b. Simples sets (2-8) have a low count. Terminal sets (1's and 9's) have a higher count.

SIMPLES				TERMINALS		
3333 Kong = 8	points	*	1111 Kong	= 16	points
333 Pung = 2	points	*	111 Pung	= 4	points
33 Pair = 0	points	*	11 Pair	= 2	points

WINDS – Only two of the winds should interest you. The dominant round wind and your seat wind. A pung of either one would double score.

WHAT TO DO

You have ONE each of the four winds. You are West and North is the round wind. Discard East and South EARLY in the play. Hopefully, no players will have a pair of their seat winds.

If you have TWO of any of the winds, hold them for a pair or possible pung. How you use them will depend upon the type of hand you're playing. Winds and dragons are not used in some the Special Hands.

DRAGONS: These three color tiles will give ANY player a score double. Discard EARLY if not needed in the structure of the hand. Otherwise, hold for a possible pung or kong double.

CONCEALED AND EXPOSED

To double the count of all sets keep them concealed in your hand as long as possible. This not only increases their value, but prevents other players from knowing what tiles are available for their use.

The only time sets have to be exposed is when they have been made from another player's discard, or for Mah Jong. Note the difference in the count:

    Concealed pung - 4-8 – points
    Exposed pung - 2-4 - points

TIPS ON PLAYING

a. Go for high count.
b. Low count – if necessary, sacrifice you hand to prevent a possible Mah Jong and having to pay out.

c. WATCH THE BOARD and which numeral tile suits are discarded by a specific player.
d. Watch what other players have exposed on their racks! Two pungs in the same suit may indicate a ONE-SUIT hand in the making. Try to avoid discarding any numeral tiles in that suit.

e. Discarding dragons – be careful. Especially late in the hand, and if none have been discarded! You may be contributing four to thirty-two points and doubling the lucky player's count.
f. Discard unneeded numeral tiles before discarding winds and dragons. You may need the honor tiles for count.

g. Develop a ONE-SUIT hand with winds and dragons. Bonus – One double.
h. Develop a ONE-SUIT hand without winds and dragons. Bonus – three doubles.

i. Count tiles! Try to avoid costly penalties.
j. If trying for a chow, use the "open-end" method.

k. If you have pairs or pungs in your hand, listen closely and respond IMMEDIATELY if a needed tile is discarded.

l. If playing a hand comprised of seven pairs, try to keep pairs of 1's and 9's, winds and dragons. This will provide you with some count in the event of Mah Jong by another player.

m. If you have a low count hand, doing this will help to limit the amount you have to pay other players. HOLD high count tiles – winds, dragons, 1's and 9's, the round wind.

n. Become familiar with a variety of the special hands for use in hand development.

o. Discard early – 1's and 9's not in your selected suit. Try to prevent another player's pung.

p. If you have a PAIR of 1's and 9's, hold early in game for a possible pung.

q. Avoid having to rely upon a wind or dragon for the needed Mah Jong tile.

r. Try to hold the "round" wind and your "seat" wind for a possible double.

s. Expose kongs of the honor tiles upon drawing them. They do not have the diversity of usage as the numeral tiles. Don't lose this count.

FLOWER PROBLEM

PROBLEM: Discovering an undeclared flower in hand <u>after</u> Mah Jong has been called.

RULE:
a. Player may not declare or count the flower, or use it for a double.
b. Hand will be considered "short" one tile and a penalty will ensue. Refer to Penalties.

PROBLEM: Discovering a flower in hand during play.

RULE:
a. When it is your regular turn, expose the flower on the rack shelf and state to the players that your are declaring an undeclared flower.
b. Draw a replacement from the Garden Wall and place it in your hand. If by chance you should draw another flower, replace this one too.
c. Take YOUR REGULAR DRAW from the Open End Wall. Discard an unneeded tile from your hand. Play continues in the usual manner.
   HOLD IT! Before discarding – do you have fourteen tiles?
   COUNT!

NOTE: An undeclared kong is handled in the same manner.

PENALTIES

With a few exceptions, the majority of the errors made during play are not correctable and require a point penalty by the player at fault.

A – MAH JONG IN ERROR
Prior to calling Mah Jong, recheck your hand before placing it on top of the rack. If exposed, all players will be aware of its makeup, and a winning hand may be difficult to acquire after a recall.

RULE:
a.   The player at fault may recall the error if NO HANDS have been exposed and resume playing.
b.   ANY exposed hands; play stops. No count.
c.   A point penalty will be imposed on the player in error. Amount – by group agreement.

B – TOO FEW TILES
a.   Error not correctable.
b.   No Mah Jong allowable.
c.   No doubles for any one-suit or honor hands.
d.   Hand count permitted.

C – TOO MANY TILES
a.   Error not correctable.
b.   No Mah Jong.
c.   No score.
d.   The other three players are paid the value of their hands.

D – FLOWER TILES
a. The undeclared flower tile is penalized as under B.
b. Cannot count the flower.
c. If a numeral tile has been declared as a flower tile, rule B will be in effect.

E – DISCARD – TILE MISCALL   (5 Bam for a 5 Dot.)

RULE:
a. If a call is made for the discard, or if tiles are exposed —50 point penalty.
b. If a call is made for Mah Jong —100 point penalty.
c. Immediate payment is made to the caller by the player at fault.
d. If no call is made, correct the error. No penalty.

The miscalled identity of a discarded tile will make it difficult for the player calling to acquire the needed set tile or the tile for Mah Jong, as the hand has been exposed.

RULE BOOK STUDY – INTERRUPTING THE PLAY

Unless there is a need for a rule verification, interrupting the play or delaying the first discard after the tiles have been drawn, should not be permitted. If it is for a "what-hand-to-play-study" – No. This affects ALL players.

a.   Play has to cease for ALL players.
b.   Concentration is lost.
c.   Disconcerting.
d.   If playing where there is a "hand-time-limit" in force – playing time is lost.

ACTION: The three remaining players continue the play three-handed. When the fourth player reenters the play, a penalty should be imposed. Amount – at the discretion of the players.

PLAYING SPEED

As soon as possible, SPEED up your playing. Your concentration and decision making will improve. You could begin in these areas.

a.   Building the wall.
b.   Drawing your tiles.
c.   Arranging your hand. Not until all tiles have been drawn.
d.   Try to decide ahead of a call what tiles you will use for discard.
e.   Discard FIRST before rearranging your hand after a draw or call.

SPECIAL HANDS

Special Hands are a challenge, adding zest to the game and have a high count. However, they are a risk in completion for Mah Jong. In instances where discards or another player's play has created havoc with your hand, try to salvage what you can by converting to a basic hand, or possibly, another special hand.

Special Hands fall in to two categories:

a. CONCEALED – All tiles have to be drawn with the exception of the one tile needed for Mah Jong, which may be drawn, or made from a player's discard.
b. EXPOSED – All tiles my be drawn or taken from a discard. Sets are made in the usual manner.
c. COUNT of the hand will be indicated as such:
   CONC. - Limit (500 points)   Half limit – 250.
   EXP. – Limit (500 points)   Half limit – 250.

Count and scoring should be clearly understood.

RULE: The limit designated will be paid to the winning hand. East Wind paying or receiving double pay.

SPECIAL HALF-LIMIT HANDS

The half-limit, 250 point hands, are handled as follows:

RULE:
a.   The hand may be doubled if players have their own seat flower, or the round flower, but only to the 500 point limit.

b.   If you Mah Jong, and do not have the seat or round double, you may add the twenty (20) point Mah Jong bonus to the 250 point score (270), and four (4) points each, for any flowers.

INCOMPLETE HANDS -- COUNTING

The incomplete one-suit-one-tile-away-from-Mah Jong hand, basic and special hands, receive a double for only the ACTUAL COUNT of the hand. Count all flowers, pungs, kongs, and pairs.

NOTE: A one-tile-away-from-Mah Jong hand with mixed suit sets of numeral tiles, is not entitled to a double.

PAIR HANDS
1. Seven pairs in one suit with winds and/or dragons. C- Limit
2. Seven pairs in on suit only. C-Limit
3. Seven pairs of mixed suits and any of the honors. C-Half Limit
4. Five pairs of one suit with NEWS. C-Limit
5. Three pairs of one suit and 6 odd honors. No. 1's & 9's. + 1 pair of honors. C-Limit

SEQUENCE HANDS
6. Sequence of 1-9 in one suit with NEWS and one wind paired. C-Limit
7. One through seven in one suit. 1 of each wind and dragon. C-Limit
8. All one suit; 2-8. 3 of each of the 1's and 9's. With any Simples paired. C-Double Limit
9. One through nine with 5 odd honors. C-Limit

CHOW HANDS
10. 3-4-5 in each suit with five odd honors. C-Limit
11. One chow of each of the suits and one of EACH wind, with one wind paired. C-Half Limit

12. One chow in EACH suit and one chow of MIXED suits with a pair of any numerals. C-Half Limit
13. 7-8-9 of EACH suit, with NEWS and one wind paired. C-Limit

HONORS – EXPOSED

14. Four pungs and one pair of terminals. Exp. Double Limit
15. Pungs or kongs of the four winds and a pair of anything.
    Exp. Double Limit
16. Four pungs and 1 pair of winds and/or dragons.
    Exp. Double Limit
17. Three pungs of dragons, 1 pung of own prevailing wind, and 1 pair of ANY wind. Exp. Triple Limit
18. Three pungs of terminals, with NEWS and 1 wind pair.
    Exp. Double Limit

HONORS - CONCEALED

19. One and nine of EACH suit, one of EACH wind and dragon with any honor or terminal paired. Con. Double Limit

20. Five pairs of 1's and 9's, with Red, White & Green dragons with one dragon paired. Con. Limit
21. Two pungs of any dragons and one pair of EACH of the winds. Con. Double Limit

MIXED SUITS

22. Three pungs of the same number in three suits, with a pung and pair of winds or pung and pair of dragons. Exp. Double Limit
23. Two pungs of same number in TWO suits, with a pair of winds or dragons. Exp. Double Limit
24. Three pungs with the same numbers in three suits, with NEWS and 1 wind paired. Exp. Double Limit
25. Run: 1-2-3 in one suit, 4-5-6 in 2nd suit, 7-8-9 in 3rd suit and five winds. C-Limit
26. Words formed from NEWS: <u>2 three letter words.</u> A pung, a chow and a pair. All in different suits. C-Limit (NEWS is made up of sixteen letter tiles.)
27. Four CONCEALED pungs and a pair using any of the three suits mixed. With or without honor tiles. C-Limit

MAH JONG – FIVE PLAYERS

ACTION: The five participants toss the dice. The lowest number becomes the Bettor. The other players take their positions at the table in the usual manner. Bettor sits out for the first hand. Following drawing of the hands, the Bettor observes each hand and places a bet on the one selected as the winner. The wind or number of the hand is noted on the Bettor Disc, placing it face down on the table during play.

RULES FOR BETTOR:
a.   Bettor does not discuss the bet.
b.   Bet may not be changed during play.
c.   Bet is disclosed following Mah Jong.
d.   A "wall game" may be bet on if Bettor feels there will not be a winner. No payment made.

SCORING AND PAYMENT:

a.   If the hand bet on wins, Bettor and winner are paid the full value of the hand.
b.   If a hand NOT bet on wins, Bettor pays full value of the hand to the winner.
c.   If East Wind is bet on and wins, ONLY EAST IS PAID DOUBLE.
d.   Bettor is subject to any penalties and pays the full value of the penalty score.

The Bettors will use their own rack and stake.

METHOD OF PLAY

<u>First Hand</u> – Bettor (sits out) makes bet on the chance of winning the game.

<u>Second Hand</u> – East gives up seat to Bettor. This will now be the North position, as the East seat moves around the table. At the end of each hand, the former East will become the Bettor, sitting out on the 2nd, 3rd, and 4th hands. East will Mah Jong only one time per hand.

ALTERNATE PLAY WITH FIVE PLAYERS

The fifth player may play without betting. The method of seating and playing would remain the same.

****

MAH JONG – THREE PLAYERS

ACTION: The three positions are East, South, and West winds. No North wind, and must be kept in this order as the East position moves around the table. The playing and scoring method is the same as for four hands. Note: No Chows may be made across the table by West and East.

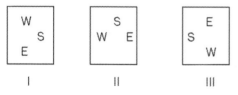

| I | II | III |

MAH JONG – TWO PLAYERS

ACTION: The players are East Wind and West Wind; sitting opposite each other. They toss the dice to determine who will be East Wind. When both players have been East, they will proceed to the second Round as in playing the four-hand game, continuing in the regular manner for the four rounds.

RULE:
a.   The Mah Jong hand must contain FOUR DOUBLES – not four pairs!
b.   No chows are permitted.
c.   Players pay each other the difference in their scores.

****

GROUP/PROGRESSIVE PLAY
With five players at the table, or when playing progressive Mah Jong, East Wind will serve in that position ONE TIME in order to limit the round to four hands.

****

TOURNAMENT PLAY
a.   East Wind will Mah Jong one time per hand.
b.   Flowers are not used.
c.   A time limit should be imposed on the play of a hand (suggested 12 minutes).

INSTRUCTOR'S OBSERVATIONS

The following observations, made over the years of teaching, indicate the common areas with which new players have problems. Bringing them to your attention may help you in developing your expertise in playing this challenging game.

a. The novice upon becoming familiar with the tiles, makeup of basic hands and the allure of the game, is interested only in playing the hand and ignoring the majority of the rules.
b. When a problem occurs, the first question is always "What do I do?" The answer is to go back and study the relative rule. Errors are not correctable. All games are played with a form of control.

ROUNDS: Students have difficulty with the structure of the Rounds and would prefer to ignore it. Why bother? The answer is that this structure forms the basis for the game action. Review the Round Section again and understand it.

BECOMING EAST: "Am I East if I Mah Jong?"
The answer is no. The East position is acquired only by rotation as this number one position moves around the table.

MAH JONG SCORE: "My score was higher than the winner's. Why am I not the winner?" The answer is the highest score is not relative to winning. Mah Jong has to meet the requirements of a basic or special hand.

SHORT HAND: Failure to draw for flower and kongs. If this occurs (especially kongs) repeatedly, the "impressive" method to correct it is by being penalized for having a "short hand;" unable to Mah Jong and having to pay the other players.
Solution: Immediately upon exposing a flower or kong, draw the replacement tile from the Garden Wall and place it on your rack. Then look at your hand and decide what to discard. NOT BEFORE!

HAND EXPOSURE: Ignoring the rule of not exposing any hands until the winner's hand has been verified as correct could result in a costly penalty for all players.

DOUBLING: Not being aware of the VALUE of the doubling process. Review count. Note: The number of times you Mah Jong will not give you the final high score. The doubling process and how you use the bonus tiles, will determine your score, high or low.

DISCARDS: Not knowing what to discard.
a.   Watch your hand and observe DISCARDED tiles. That is the
      purpose for their face up position on the table.

b. Observe sets exposed on racks.
c. Discarding winds? Ask yourself, what is my Seat wind? What is the Round Wind?
d. If you have a pair to discard, don't discard them in succession. Wait for several turns.
e. Hold any obvious tiles that you feel will give you Mah Jong. Sacrifice your hand if necessary.

MOST COMMON ERRORS
a. Failure to draw for kongs. (Popular!)
b. Overlooking doubles.
c. Not being familiar with the rules.
d. Incorrect count of Special Hands.
e. Exposing hand when Mah Jong is declared by another player.
f. Disregarding the "rotation" rule when paying off at the end of the hand. Confusion ensues.

NOTE: In order to expedite your learning process, study the following basic areas:
a. Become familiar with the structure and variety of the basic hands.
b. COUNT! This cannot be overemphasized. Not just at the end of the hand, while playing and discarding. A dragon tile, punged, will give ANY player a double score. A wind tile discard will only double the score of the player occupying that particular seat position.

NO -- NO'S -- IT'S EVERY PLAYER - SOLO!

The concept of the good neighbor policy is not permissible in the game of Mah Jong. Aiding may impose a penalty from one or more players. The amount, by group agreement.

- You do not handle another player's tiles.
- You do not assist a player in playing their hand.
- You do not ask a player if they have drawn for their initial flower or for future flowers.
- You do not remind a player to draw for a kong or a flower. This is a penalty error.
- You do not hand a player a replacement tile for a kong or flower. They are points!
- You do not assist a player in counting their hand. (Count it to yourself.)
- You do not alert a player of an "under" count of their hand. This is their problem. You will be penalized by the other players.
- If a player has "over-counted" the hand, this error must be corrected prior to payments. No penalty imposed for this alert.

OOPS ERRORS!

a. Declaring a numeral tile as a flower – penalty.
b. Failing to draw for a flower tile – penalty.
c. Failing to draw for a kong – penalty.
d. Not declaring a kong prior to Mah Jong.
e. Breaking the wall from left. Make correction.
f. Failing to immediately declare a flower garden. (Blew 3,000 points. Big Oops!)
g. Failing to add the 20 point bonus for Mah Jong.
h. Exposing hand as soon as another player declares Mah Jong. Could lose your count!
i. Missing the call for a pung or kong.
j. Failing to make a kong of your exposed pung upon drawing the fourth like tile.
k. Failing to add the two points for a pair.
l. Failing to double for a pung or kong of dragons.
m. Failing to double for your seat wind.
n. Failing to double for your seat flower.
o. Failing to double for the round wind.
p. Failing to double for the round flower.

Remember, you're only human – No penalty!

****

FINAL WORD

I do not claim expert status in having shared this information with you, as you and I will continue to learn with every hand played.

****

One of the most important tips: Insist on little or no conversation. Concentration is a must in playing Mah Jong.

 ---- **ENJOY IT!**

Printed in the United States
By Bookmasters